The Observation of Basic Matter

John Cullen

𝄢

Bass Clef Books
Cecilia, KY

First Edition

ISBN
ISBN: 979-8-9898478-4-6

$15.00

Bass Clef Books is an imprint of MARZEK Publishing
Mick Kennedy, Publisher

Acknowledgements

"Should We Do It Again" in *Concho River Review*

"The Three-Legged Race" in *The MacGuffin*

"Outside Limits" in *Sky Island Journal*

"Halloween," in *Hole in the Head*

"Heritage" in *Pembroke*

"Seventh Grade Math" in *Main Street Rag*

"The Planets" in *Moon City Review*

"Observation of Basic Matter" in *Book of Matches*

"Travelling Home" in *ithacalit*

"Privacy" in *North Dakota Quarterly*

"Stingray" in *Cleaver*

"At Chemo" in *Orchard Press*

"The Eyes are the Door" in *Hamilton Stone Review*

"The Promise" in *Rockvale Review*

"Late Night Phone Call" in *I-70*

"Town Song" in *American Journal of Poetry*

"Jogging" in *Cincinnati Poetry Review*

"The Internet Tells Us" in *Change Seven*

"My Russian Autobiography" in *Poems and Plays*

Table of Contents

Should We Do It Again

No wonder we fumbled rather than cuddled,
ran the kickoff out of the end zone
rather than hugged the touchback,
spiked the ball and ate a penalty to dance
rather than take a knee and nibble the Holy Ghost.
It all comes back to that rope in gym class,
the one that almost no one could climb
except the athletic few, gifted like chimps,
monkeying up to touch the ceiling.
No wonder we raced without a helmet,
drove like a fool around hairpin turns
on the road that circled the county dump.
I remember our science teacher, Mr. Johnson,
describing gravity in an ordered universe.
A planet broken from orbit, he warned us,
spun through the void till sucked in by the sun
to a fiery splash in an ocean of fusion.
The velocity of impact plus nuclear fusion
would explode with the force of a million
million Fat Boys over Nagasaki.
Here on earth no one would feel the impact
or witness the dance of blazing atoms.
That same afternoon we ditched Spanish.
My best friend's father had given him the Malibu
and the keys crouched heavy in his pocket.
Beneath the music, we felt the pull, rounding
the curve of county road seven, all our weight
straining our orbit, pulling us close to the county dump
with the explosive force of atomizing hormones,
nothing but rubber between us and the nearest sun.

Outside Limits

Barely outside
city limits, we slipped
the Plymouth along-
side a Russian olive hedge
at Kramer Lane overlook
for the kiss of adolescent
fumbling that was all
thumbs and rough fabrics
crashing one another.   Sometimes
we peered across the water, unsure why
but intuiting that distance
meant possibility.   All we had
stretched and snapped.

One afternoon, a cloud bank
stormed up the river,
rolling over itself and more
threatening than summer's
latest special effects.
We paused as lightning forked
water below the bridge,
and we imagined
fish paralyzed
by that swift jolt. We adjusted straps,
zipped our jeans and rubbed
love's vapor off the window,
then plunged, reckless once
again, back to the city, the storm's
stab and churn
inside us.

Halloween

Lawns orange in the porch light, that punk smell
of wet leaves, three days before Halloween,
we crouched behind privets and picket fences
to scout the neighborhood, lurking behind Chevys
in gravel driveways, primed to release. Saturated with sugar
and the gum of destruction we peeked through
windows at black and white television shadows
across living room walls, or crept outside a kitchen
to catch someone's sister lick salt from the popcorn bowl
while she talked on the phone and stole her mother's smokes.
Usually, we juiced ourselves to smash pumpkins.
One of us dared the others to spy on Mr. Winser,
a bullet-headed man who worked at the Mobile factory
pressing egg cartons and chased his kids if they failed
to make curfew before the stuttering streetlights called night,
whipping them home with his belt. Crew cut flatter
than "Because I told you so," he hunched in his basement,
and we watched through the window well.
A Bud Light in one hand, he loosened brake
parts, worn pads and rotors, the torque and bleeder
beside him. His wife staggered hauling the laundry basket
with a burping towel asleep on her shoulder.

I wish we had witnessed a tender scene.
Man and woman at the foundation of their home
while upstairs the kids watched Black Christmas, unwrapped
mummy costumes, and planned prize-winning staggers.
They could have embraced, but that dark dog
who snarled behind fences and menaced us after school
running unleashed through the neighborhood
left the woman who baked us cupcakes crying.
We twisted the tails of a few Black Cats, lit the fuse and left
the sputter on his concrete ledge. We ran wild
through the neighborhood maze, past ghosts and skeletons,
that barking hound and swaggering pirates, listening
for explosions, not understanding the shards that flew.

Heritage

"Others composted, we ate soup,"
my father joked. "One egg plus margarine
instead of the recipe's three and butter.
Very little slipped those thin fingers."
After she passed, we gathered to page
her diary. A family of nurses and one pilot,
insurance agent and teachers, a barbed wire artist,
three John Deeres and two hundred acres.
The diary stacked two inches, seed and detail
scripted on onion skin, the paper
remaindered at the five and dime.

Seventh Grade Math

Because in math I always sat behind Deirdre
    Bugbee, C coming after B, with no one between
        the two of us, true as lovers.

Because I could never do math as long as her hair
rushed into a ponytail. Because Mr. Green called role
        then wrote equations on the board in yellow chalk.

Because during math detention, he became so frustrated
    he left the room and never returned, so we went home.
        Because the next day he stopped before writing

the equation and cried, shoulders shaking, facing the board,
    the yellow chalk gripped in his right hand,
        his sobs so ragged no one dared breathe.

Because Mrs. Clark came into the room, spoke softly
    then walked him off like a player injured on the field.
        Because Mrs. Clark returned and solved a problem.

Because the next day Mr. Green appeared the same
    as ever, yellow chalk in hand, and wrote a problem
        on the board as if nothing had happened.

Because when Mr. Green stopped writing on the board
    he called my name, "Earth to Cullen," like NASA
        might have radioed John Glenn in space.

Because everyone laughed, and Deirdre Bugbee looked.
    Because Mr. Green didn't laugh, then called my first name
        and said, "Let's work the problem, step by step."

The Planets

The nine planets strained wires
attached to the ceiling, spaced accordingly,
the universe scaled to the length of our class.
Attention on the heavens, I sat second
in the fourth row, directly under Mars.
Today, I stare at that photograph
my mother snapped after delivering cupcakes.
Debbie Gilmore seated on my right,
blue blazer and starched white
button down collar. Mrs. Johnson
stood behind us, one hand pressing
on each shoulder, momentarily
balancing planetary forces.
Each of us looks straight ahead,
the moment barely capturing the strain
in our jittering orbits, our future
divorces and attractions tracing
meteoric paths from distant universes.

Travelling Home

We stuffed luggage under leather
seats that looked like benches from Trudy's Café,
circa 1950. The Lake Shore Express
shrugged off Toledo, rattling across soy
fields, slowing at every cross road in Ohio
and up the west end of Pennsylvania. Amtrak overbooked.
Heaters broken so passengers crowded
into the kitchen car to munch on Wonder
Bread and American cheese, eager
to keep what heat they could. Two days before Christmas,
everyone rushing home. And old man, drunk
on beer and good will, repeated
this advice: "You've got to do it on your own!"
He ground his fist in his palm as if compounding
a poultice to draw infection. A clear night outside
the viewing window. Moonlight glittered snow and the few
cars along rural roads. We waited one hour
on a siding in Cleveland. It was as quiet
as the week before creation. No angel in wool coat
and fedora rode those rails to show us the error
of our ways. The exhale of doors in Erie
brought no ghosts. Outside Buffalo,
with the kitchen closed and the porter dozing, diehards
in the viewing car examined warm beer cans.
There was no house in sight, and the train clanked
past a horse and rider dragging a pine,
as the dark engine pulled us further north,
closer to home. We loosened wool scarves
from around our necks. Someone snored, and an infant
brought on one stop beyond Erie wrapped heavily
against the weather burped once,
a perfect bubble on pink lips.

Puzzle

Even during chemistry, my sister
strummed chords, fingers
caressing frets or stretching
strings bleeding the blues.
Sometimes she'd pick
a country tune, wailing for lost
beers and pickup trucks,
mourning every orphan.
Now her fingers pluck
bibs and diapers
from laundry, her kids
a Greek chorus of woes
and triumphs. The guitar resonates
during birthdays
and family gatherings.
My brother-in-law puzzles
after beers
one night, confessing
she hums in her sleep,
and taps fingers.
It's weird, he tells me:
sometimes one hand
finds a rhythm, as if
stroking our last
dog's head.

Jigsaw

He'd always ridden.
Then a gelding spooked, tossing him
after the fighter jet rattled the metal roof.
Foot trapped in one stirrup, he dragged
for thirty yards, kicked twice in the head.
I visited the nursing home.
In the recreation room, a ghost in a flowered
house dress worked a jigsaw, recreating
the painting on a puzzle box, white farmhouse, rocker
on porch, corn broom leaning and leather gloves shaking hands.
Severe disruption in the posterior cingulate cortex.
The following week, I signed in again, a new puzzle
on the table. The Himalayans? A half completed sky.

We believe we can order the jigsaw. Simple puzzles
we offer the young, but they outgrow the table
and pieces chase life. His sister and I embraced
the last time I attended, then walked together
through reception. Mount Rushmore towered
above pine and granite. Chin resting on spotted hands
folded over his cane, a man lost in his shirt stared
at the scattered pieces. There was no hope or chance
to visit, the machine's gasps unplugged, and only memory.
Others continue to work the puzzle. We can't stop
fitting pieces, nudging each shape to mate, trying
to order that smallest world, despite the jumble outside
the jig-cut border.

Privacy

The hospice worker phoned,
delayed.
Again
at another client's home. Waiting
at the window, my mother wonders
what happened. I know
but don't want to
tell her.

           "Oh,
maybe the rain
slowed her down?" This morning
we're alone.
I will have to change
her sweat-damp shirt, the second
since she woke at five.
"Is it snowing?" she asks.
Outside, it's ninety.

I hate to do this, and feel
embarrassed
for her, and uneasy
at the sight of her
shrunken breasts,
which reminds me
how life pulls in on itself
near the end. She eases
back into her wheelchair,
and I roll the TV
volume up
while I try to disengage
her hairclip.

"Oh, dear." She feels
everything coming undone
as her hair spills
down her shoulders, and all
I can do is coil it behind
her neck, like a limp rope,
and reassure her
I will braid her hair
after we change
her shirt.

I'll give her one
of my V-neck T's
with a flowery spray.
They go over her head
loosely, the smell reminding her
of her father, who after
each morning's shave splashed her
with cologne. The fresh cotton
wicks her anxiety.

I prepare to remove her shirt.
She sits clutching
my white T,
inhaling her past. I stand
behind the wheelchair
for privacy. "Wait!"
she commands.
"I don't want Nate Berkus to see me naked!"

Stingray

My sister and I recall that old Stingray
while we sit a vigil in the critical care unit.
She melts into the vinyl cushions
and I lean sideways, balanced like a circus
acrobat one moment before falling.
My bike rolled sweet, balanced
on training wheels I begged my father to remove.
He wouldn't lift a wrench without my mother's consent.
Even Steve Reeves could not have popped a wheelie!
Then, one day he disengaged the pair,
and I rode to the park, where on a dare
from Nancy Haver I jackknifed
a set of concrete steps, snapped off my front
tooth and broke my right arm.
My sister dragged me home while I cried
over my broken bike. She laughs at the memory,
which reminds her, she says, of another story.

Just then our mother shakes
the bedside railing, angry at being jailed,
and calls again our father's name.
"When will he be back?" She cries.
From my side of the bed, I lift her cup
and guide the polka dot straw to her lips
while my sister punches morphine
and holds her other hand to clamp the pain.
Later, she wakes, and once again
bangs the railing, this time
pulling her oxygen line free,
but the nurse arrives and tapes the tubing.
Exhausted, we slump, almost asleep. She turns
on her side, trying to find comfort
and our father, each of us seeking
balance on the body's edge.

At Chemo

One waiting spouse, discouraged
chinos and a chili stain
ballooning through the sky
blue of his shirt where a belly
should extend, repeatedly rubs
one hand over his bristled head,
as if conjuring a crystal
ball to locate hope.

Likely, he shaved his noggin
to blend with his wife's
loss. A vague guilt at being
healthy bends his anger.
A teenage girl shrugs inside her leather
jacket studded with spikes
and chains, registers at the sliding window,
slumps on the plastic couch.
A green streak in her
wisp of hair flares beneath the Muzak,
as if a jumper yelled "Bonzai!"
before jackknifing off a cliff
into shark infested waters.
When they look at each other, something
passes between them. The man smiles
then nods, and she grins.
For a moment they could embrace
like family members.
If they did, perhaps their struggling
wings would embrace their racing hearts

The Eyes are the Door

    She's licked death for two days, and we breathe
softly, checking for the signs.
Cold toes, hospice tell us, means shutdown
of major organs. She is cushioned against
the coming storm in a morphine snowsuit .

    "She has found the door and is ready
to step through." That's what the nurse says.
I imagine a huge set of revolving glass
doors like the ones outside a bank.
Some people enter and some exit, nodding
as they pass. By afternoon, her toes feel cold.

    If it is a glass revolving door and she is half-
way in with no possibility of return
can she look back through the panes
and see us standing here? Confusing,
isn't it? Likely she sees our mouths
open and close, strange fish gasping behind glass.

What Can I Do?

The hospice nurse arrives, consults
the computer, determines my mother
needs oxygen. She writes
the order. The traveling doctor
arrives to monitor her
heart. I invite him inside
and watch.

He listens carefully, says
"breathe deeply", then marks her chart. Later,
a stranger from Urgent Care wheels in
the oxygen machine,
and another stranger fills out
paperwork on a clipboard,
while I stand off
to one side, not sure
which line to sign. I wonder
what I can do to help.

Plastic tubing unwinds
from sterile packing, connectors
snug over brass nipples, and a canister
filled with distilled water preserves her lips
and lungs from drying out. Foam
dresses the tubing for sensitive ears.
And I wonder what I can do,

and then the machine beeps.
Three lights go on. Then two fade.
One will hum all night. The technician clarifies
my concern should be the green, the only
one which should never go out.
If that one fails, it's warning me
to call the number on the sticker.
I wonder what I can do,

so they show me
how to clean the tube. Everyone departs
except the two of us, and the machine
shudders, then belches oxygen, which passes
through tubing, then more tubing
leaking from the claw-like nose piece.

The Promise

Crows push a black arrow over pine hills.
Simmentals trace the path to the paddock.
The last young bull clowns, kicking up heels,
shaking his head like he inhaled pepper.
The day is a lifetime when the pasture is green.
I stand on the porch cradling this clay urn
my mother turned on her wheel. Her thrown pots,
building beauty from mud, surrounded nothing
but empty space. This is the second day
I can't fulfill my promise to spread her ashes.

Observation of Basic Matter

The lump in my sister's
breast, pea-shaped,
caused a flood.
My father, shocked
by force of relation,
wouldn't emit a sound.
My sisters talked
in whispers, believing
words and touch leaven
the fear. Doctors puzzled
cell margins, semi-regular
at best, not enough
to convince them cancer
had not spread.

In the end, the cancer was
both there and not
there, that old
quantum dilemma.
Radiation, recommended
one, but not the other.
She received treatment,
and clumps of blue
streaked hair fell out.
All I could say was,
"Why not just shave it?"

But there are courses
to these forces. Colorful
scarves, wigs and jokes
mixed a synergy I couldn't
understand.
Now yearly checkups
seek rogue cells.
My sisters negotiate
relations, health a ritual.
The men of the family sputter
like cold fusion experiments.
Distant planets visible
in the needy twilight, old
men circle in lonely
Newtonian orbits.

Late Night Phone Call

A friend who works a suicide hotline phones me
on an October evening. Just as maple leaves turn
orange and fall, our talk turns to the red
of personal lives, which often leads to winter
confusion. His wife is leaving him for a floral decorator.
He always thought the guy was gay. Turns out he's not,
and owns an American Marine yacht docked in Ludington
on which, daily, he's been shucking her
like an oysterman. His words, not mine.
He and his wife raised two pearls, and all those years
ate boatloads of oatmeal. They nursed the dream
of a trip to Rome, to visit the Sistine Chapel
and stretch their fingers to God and grace. Somehow
their baggage prevented travel. "And what's that worth
now," he wants to know, angry and confused.
There's nothing more puzzling than a suitcase
with one pair of someone else's underwear
in the elastic laundry pocket. My words, not his.
I shared an apartment with a philosophy major
who twirled pasta while discussing Wittgenstein.
Mac and cheese all we could afford. After a year
of arguing over who failed to pay the electric
and who first claimed space in the basement
we decided it was time to divide the furniture.
Now I sit listening to my friend, who has found himself
shipwrecked on an island, walking a private beach.
Both of us make our livings unsnarling
words, trying to trace the string and tease each knot.
He studies the tracks and scribbles in the sand
where gulls and driftwood write a parting note.

Paris Fish Pond

A quarter clicks, and a woman scatters corn
pellets across the water. Glistening
scales churn, like an Ur-python coiling
the planet, as fish mouths kiss and slurp.
Tourists step back in awe, Mon Dieu!
Cellphones click. Before smooth waters return,
an amazed child reaches to touch scales,
but they've disappeared.
He casts his mother's remaining pellet
into the depths, believing a single fish
rising to the lure will reveal its face,
and leans forward, so close to the surface,
he almost falls into algae and fin.
His parents pull him from the pool's lip,
bushwhacked by mystery as fish
nibble the meniscus. Some people
read twisted sheds as prophetic
of changing seasons, shakeups in odds.
Others sense the sexual touch of astral
bodies reaching from lonely rotations.
My grandmother insisted rain and frogs
promise mushrooms under the kitchen sink.
We keep trying to read the text
of our world, to learn beyond prejudice,
but like the couple in the newspaper
who let a stray dog sleep on the bed
until he ripped their infant's face
as he slept under a sky-blue blanket
of logic, we keep getting eaten.
There's no insurance policy against the gods' whims.
We continue, pausing on occasion, to witness
fish boiling cold waters or lunging upstream
to spawn then relax to death. Flesh flakes
and settles, like chalk sentences drifting
off the school board. We can't lift our eyes
from the world and whatever roils through
darkness into myth. The world whispers
not of what was lost but of what might be
without our ever knowing it.

Town Song

You might recall a certain spot, say the arbor
near the river, heavy with concords spotted
from the willows where you and your friends dashed
and grabbed, surprised by the resiliency of twisted stems,
amazed by the mist of grape skin on a fall morning,
and terrified by the snarling shepherd launched from the barn.
Sluggish bullheads in the lake's north end mumbled midnight
verse while locals joked about angling bait, and carp rolled golden
in afternoon sun. You tossed your line a mile beyond them,
as if casting your spoon over a passing freighter, reeling quickly
to feel the weight.

Now it's concrete, maybe a factory,
with bark chip mounds surrounding miniature bushes. The grounds
crew clips hedges with an electric trimmer sounding nothing like cicada
in evening elms, while tractors and skidders brush cut every lawn.
The brochure announces Happy Harbor, a dock and boat
for every condo. There's never a beagle chasing rabbits
through morning mists, just the sagging rainbow of oily bilge
sneaking across water from the boat launch bay while bulldozers gasp
in the farthest corner and strip rich soil for a privacy hill.

You can only dream the places that hurt, the times
you cried or tried your best to be a man. Say, the thirty foot hickory
in the school's back lot. You remember one kiss burning two
names in bark. Or that rundown stucco with a Harley in the alley,
the only one around. A thin girl made you brave but was called back
by the moon. People walking by can't hear your name,
and for all you know arrived from Venus. They don't remember
the Braves, down by twenty but rallying with a sand lot hitch-and-go,
and there isn't a waitress who can pull a cherry phosphate.

It's no longer your town, and smiles
are gangsters, and it's no consolation you know they'll lose it too,
their family land disgraced by concrete, their neighborhood park
reduced to tar then cut in lots for a brand new Speedy Seven.
Like a song you heard one dusty summer and would call
your own if you could hum just one more bar, your town shimmers
then disappears from sight, like highway lakes the tires never reach.
It's not your town and never was. Growing old means learning
the truth: your town belongs to no one. It doesn't exist,
though you stand in its midst and breathe in every place.

The Three-Legged Race

Newly wed, my wife and I owned
nothing. In a rented attic apartment
over the B&K liquor store, heat blustered
all summer, and the troll next door controlled
winter with a flip of the thermostat
nailed on the wall under her bridge.
We panned garage sales for spatulas and spoons,
wrestled saggy couches, snagged a leather chair
filled with dog hair, popcorn, and pennies.
We started a collection of marbles and glass eyes.
Our kitchen table, free that summer, limped home
on three legs. With duct tape, screw, bolt,
and one metal crutch, we attached a fourth leg.
Suddenly, the table served four, plates seated.
Patterns swirled in the varnished top, messages
like the tea leaves our new age landlord pondered.
We lacquered the living room floor bright red.
Then we got married again, and again. First to jobs,
then to a new Ford, and divided our universe
between neighbors and families, kids and a lawn,
then new socks and shoes, then pencils and litter boxes.
When the kids invited friends, we ordered pizza
then paid for a pool, cell phones, a tent,
then a four year stay at State, and fake testicles
for our neutered retriever. Teenagers
we didn't recognize snored and borrowed towels.
Finally, kids migrated and the goldfish resigned,
and once again it was the two of us eating muffins
from an organic bakery with Cuban coffee,
marveling butter swirls on cornbread.
We decided to return to the wild hunt,
a quest of sorts for the three-legged table, just the way
it was from that very first day, that day
we married for the first time.

Jogging

If I tell my neighbor I'm going out to run
for half an hour, he asks me where I'm going,
really. As if I had secretly parked my car
somewhere around the block and intend to drive
to a destination I refuse to name in public.
I keep insisting I'm just running for the blood.
Not really going anywhere. Just jogging, you know, for my health.
"Mow the lawn! Get a real job! Paint the house!" He grins.

The pros stride by me, regular and thin,
with blue stripes zigzagged along each sneaker and athletic
T-shirts plastered to backs by miles and miles of sweat.
To them I'm going nowhere fast. Though at least,
they would admit, I'm headed in the right direction.
My wife waits, sketch pad in hand, convinced of nothing
and expecting me soon---because I'm reverting to childhood---
to purchase a mitt and chalk a strike zone on the barn.

This is a journey for the blood, I tell myself,
at this point not sure exactly what I mean, but aware
that somehow the more I say it the more it sounds quite true.
My oldest soon hoots, "Then you won't need the car
later tonight! So I can take it to the movies and then
to the bar before making a spin down Steven's Road?"
He wiggled his eyebrows and tipped some ash,
and for a minute I picture him on his own trip for blood!

But sometimes when calling the spurt toward home,
just for the moment, I forget my age, the way jazz on the radio
while I drive at night makes me forget about the car.
And for that moment, I could run forever, not really going,
not really coming, as the world goes by while I tread water.
But then there's the ache, the pain in the gut and sweat,
the everyday weight that makes me recognize the body
as the poor second cousin I know it's meant to be.

Rounding the corner, I spot my neighbor's head
bent to inspect a Dorthy Perkins, anxious over pruning
so as not to bruise cane. Measuring phosphate,
compost and ash, he's afloat in Hugona, floribunda and Blaze,

28

the way running for the blood makes imagination's sense.
I imagine the spiral down after flight, the sudden erase
and then break through cloud. Solid on ground,
bump and rumble, I taxi slowly toward home.

The Internet Tells Us

"Plastic Surgeons hate this woman,"
who reversed aging, reduced lap and sag
then forced the crows to drop corn and fly home.
She bypassed the laser gang and knife
to fashion an umbrella against life's storm
defying the cosmic order, compounding
pharmaceuticals and organic foods in a blender,
then painting her face with avocado mash.
Once the mask arrested wrinkles and feet,
she peeled the gummy eraser, her skin smooth,
nude in the bathroom mirror. We long to believe
relief promised from the tragedy of gravity's slip and slide.
So bring on the chemical revelations! We're ready
for whatever scares birds or slows death's escalator.
This is our religion, a tree that offers shade to save life
and line, and calls us to worship regardless of its roots.
Let's face it; we're nuts. We can't stop striving
to schnooker Father Time, though we know the body
flows in one direction, undercutting banks and tickling silt.

Somewhere in South America

Today must be the first
day of jungle summer, and a headhunter
must be crouching in front of a fire, filling
an enemy's head with hot coals and sand, sewing
the eyelids shut and knotting the pursed lips with thread.

Down the path, his three
children drink stream water, then gut
a brown lizard to spice the soup while his wife,
or maybe his second wife, repairs the roof's thatching
by layering dried sheaves of brown savanna sweet grass.

I'm going to believe this, not just because I made it up,
or because I fantasize about bigamy each day I trudge to work,
or because I love the smell of braided summer sweet grass,
or because I swiped a shrunken head from the local museum's
shelf,
but because of the need to believe in something

we don't know, some blood-based charm warding
black and white magics, some cure-all herbal or fairy tale
balm, a father in the sky, a molecule's wings, the rocket's thrust
or our babble in darkness, whatever gives security
in this world, of which we can't be sure.

One Vote

"Hummingbirds, maybe, but" one hand up
to pause, "they're invasive, mess up everything.
…kind of like you." Smiles….. but only half means it.
A grizzled guy in a USN New Mexico cap
hovered over anemic seedlings at station two.
I almost asked him to vote, but the way he gripped
a walking stick with a crow-head carved top…
Katy's Kustom Plants. Blue poly Nike sweats,
matching wind breaker, sneakers, three grey braids,
she discusses vinegar traps. It's too exciting
so next a wiry guy, dirty tee, clearing his throat.
Must be the aphidian oracle.
Just one damn trumpet vine to scrabble life
up the weathered barn, sneak under rafters
and blast knotholes, an apostle of blossoms.
Both sides sun and runoff,
it would thrive, bother no one, at best shock
a lonely driver who'd seen Deliverance
and regretted his scenic way home plan.
"You miss the point," insists my wife,
bringing us back to the present tense.
"Why don't you dig up a hotdog (her idea
of a joke) while I dig up some caladium."
Naturally, I trailed off to my people
between the parked cars, all those dandelions
and tangled pigweed punching through blacktop.

Of Toads

Bees brew dark
honey, this time of year
flavored with the spice
aster and goldenrod.
My wife juggles the weight
of supers and winter needs, exactly
what makes me nervous.
I'm comfortable around bees,
but need the smoker
puffing them to gorge
before I check for mites
or restrict entry from wind.
It's the killing of the drones
that worries me, the idea
those who swagger and swig
must be driven over the edge
in preparation for hard times
without supper. I imagine
the banished. Antennas bent,
three legs wrenched, one of many eyes
poked, little punching bags stutter-buzzing,
hoping no hungry toads
crouch below the boards.
Having served their function,
they're downsized.
It's true that some
of us simply aren't useful,
except in moments
of passion or sketching trees.

Like frosting, we're not a meal
but everyone's favorite.
I worry we're first to go
before hard winter,
when bees tap capped cells.
Instead, let's steep sweet tea,
uncork strong spirits, and raise
a toast to fallen friends,
then sit back and rest,
while I tell a story

about honey, blossoms,
and red zinger tea,
all the parts necessary
to survive harsh winters.

My Russian Autobiography

I know by now, had I been born a Kirghiz,
I would have hailed from Chuy
in the north of Kyrgyzstan, born to peasants
whose Turkic twists the tongue.

And it's clear to me now
that I'd have been the village idiot,
baking bread at the bakery for the local rich
and considered a success to have remembered hat and wage.

In this life I married, but seldom drink vodka.
I've never gone skating with a girl named Anna
and seldom seen wolves prowling outside the flock,
despite wintering last year in northern Michigan.

But I know death's sack, the struggle and loss,
that war is horrible and brothers shouldn't quarrel,
that skating's OK when the ice grows thick.
My outlook's romantic, some would say simple.

So, remember me well. I'm the village idiot!
I rely on kindness and would never hurt a dog.
I've baked today's bread! I've remembered my hat!
The oven's still warm and my dear mother loves me.

About the Author

John Cullen graduated from SUNY Geneseo. He worked with a talent agency booking rock bands, a clown troupe, and an R-rate magician. He went back to school and graduated from BGSU. He has taught literature and writing at Ferris State University for many years and currently lives in West Michigan. His work has appeared in magazines such as *Harpur Palate, Pembroke Magazine, New York Quarterly,* and *South Florida Poetry Journal.* His poem "Curing" is an honorable mention in the Passager 2025 poetry contest, and his poem "Appeasement" won the 2022 Street Light Magazine Poetry award. His first chapbook, *Town Crazy,* is available from Slipstream Press.